Why can't ostriches fly?

Written by Mary Roulston

Illustrated by Rose Wilkinson

Collins

What's in this book?

Listen and say

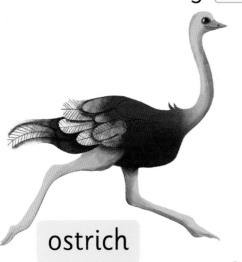

ostrich

emperor penguin

peacock

Download the audio at www.collins.co.uk/839782

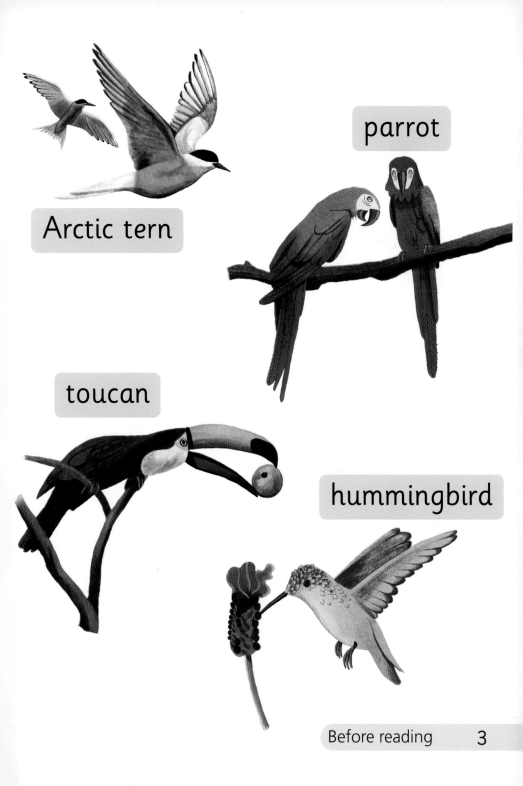

parrot

Arctic tern

toucan

hummingbird

Ostriches have got big bodies and long legs, but their wings are small. They can't fly. They're too big!

wing

They can't fly, but they can run very fast.

These birds are emperor penguins.

They can't fly, but they are very good at swimming.

These birds are peacocks.
They can fly, but not very well.

They have beautiful tails.

tail

These are Arctic terns.
They can fly very well!

They fly 70 000 km a year! Wow!

These are hummingbirds.
They're very small. They've got
a lot of colours and long beaks.

beak

Hummingbirds can fly. They move their wings very fast.

These birds are parrots.
They fly up into big trees.

Parrots can open nuts with
their beaks.

nut

These birds have got big beaks, too.
These birds are toucans. They have
got lots of colours on their big beaks.

Toucans can fly. A big beak does not stop them.

What bird do you like?
Can it fly or not? Can it swim?
Can it run fast?

Has it got short or long wings?
Has it got a long tail? Has it got
a big beak?

Picture dictionary

Listen and repeat

beak

bird

fly

run

swim

tail

wings

1 Look and match

Arctic tern

emperor penguin

peacock

parrot

ostrich

2 Listen and say

Collins

Published by Collins
An imprint of HarperCollins*Publishers*
Westerhill Road
Bishopbriggs
Glasgow
G64 2QT

HarperCollins*Publishers*
1st Floor, Watermarque Building
Ringsend Road
Dublin 4
Ireland

William Collins' dream of knowledge for all began with the publication of his first book in 1819.

A self-educated mill worker, he not only enriched millions of lives, but also founded a flourishing publishing house. Today, staying true to this spirit, Collins books are packed with inspiration, innovation and practical expertise. They place you at the centre of a world of possibility and give you exactly what you need to explore it.

© HarperCollins*Publishers* Limited 2020

10 9 8 7 6 5 4 3 2

ISBN 978-0-00-839782-1

www.collins.co.uk/elt

British Library Cataloguing in Publication Data

A catalogue record for this publication is available from the British Library.

Author: Mary Roulston
Illustrator: Rose Wilkinson (Beehive)
Series editor: Rebecca Adlard
Commissioning editor: Zoë Clarke
Publishing manager: Lisa Todd
Product managers: Jennifer Hall and Caroline Green
In-house editor: Alma Puts Keren
Project manager: Emily Hooton
Editor: Tessie Papadopoulou-Dalton
Proofreaders: Natalie Murray and Michael Lamb
Cover designer: Kevin Robbins
Typesetter: 2Hoots Publishing Services Ltd
Audio produced by id audio, London
Reading guide author: Emma Wilkinson
Production controller: Rachel Weaver
Printed and bound by: GPS Group, Slovenia

MIX
**Paper from
responsible sources**

FSC
www.fsc.org

FSC™ C007454

Download the audio for this book and a reading guide for parents and teachers at www.collins.co.uk/009702